Après

Lauri Robertson

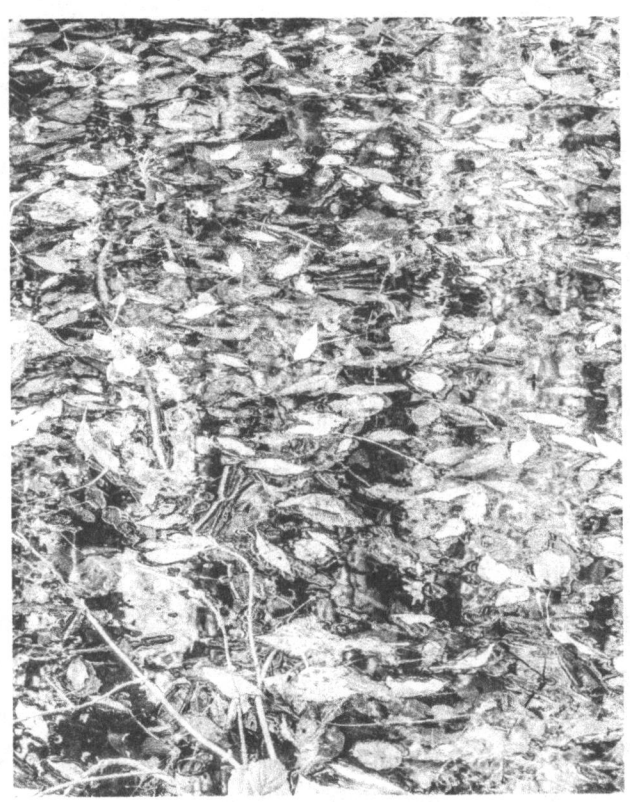

SPUYTEN DUYVIL
New York City

ISBN 978-1-956005-74-5

Cover photo by the author, "Pontlevoy Ruisseau, 2020"

Library of Congress Cataloging-in-Publication Data

Names: Robertson, Lauri Rosemary, author.
Title: Après / Lauri Robertson.
Description: New York City : Spuyten Duyvil, [2022]
Identifiers: LCCN 2022027645 | ISBN 9781956005745 (paperback)
Subjects: LCGFT: Novels.
Classification: LCC PS3618.O316978 A67 2022 | DDC 813/.6--dc23/eng/20220624
LC record available at https://lccn.loc.gov/2022027645

In her expansive 4th monograph, *Après*, Lauri Robertson offers poems that are baldly, powerfully sincere, and others said with a wink. The year 2020 finds her in a neglected garden feeling overwhelmed by George Floyd's death: *We come here to love/all we've ever loved, to reach beyond/anything we've ever touched or seen/or to do nothing but sit among crazy vines.* The protests have been "spring-loaded" by the pandemic, and she chastises herself to *Speak up, white woman. What will you say?* The topical is, however, a layered, complex matrix of the intimate and universal. To amplify, interrogate, or contain emotion there are surprising turns if not moments of whiplash, like cats who *...suddenly/ need to groom, a fine/displacement (for all of us).* With sustained gestures of gravity, wit and affection, Robertson gives us *...light/crossing one's eyelids/as if touch, rendering/the story of who/we really are.*

      Danielle McNally

In *Après*, Lauri Robertson takes the reader on familiar and companionable tours—revisiting marriage, her menagerie (hedgehog, bat, rabbit, fish, and forever cats), our bodies, and coming to the end. Yet there is more. From an abandoned garden in a French village, she gives voice in call-and-response to the shocks après the pandemic and the killing of George Floyd. "The Secret Garden" poems bring to mind the hortus conclusus of the Middles Ages, here a transitional space between lyric and public. The personal and political are entwined as the poet pays her respects to Toni Morrison and Adrienne Rich. Throughout the collection, Robertson's candor and asides to herself and the reader hold us close to her poetic voice.

      Nancy Olson

Robertson's intriguing new volume of delightful and challenging thoughts and memories speaks to one's singular heart. Darting from the cauldron of COVID to the secret world of nature and animals, on to issues of #BLM and through the essence of language and thought, she captures our imagination. Her poems are bold, nuanced, and wise. Carefully crafted rage, bereavement, humor, and echoes of progenitors abound. Robertson's work can be deceptively plain spoken or natively highbrow. She is, in essence, a 'poet's poet' both passionate and bemusedly skeptical about her own endeavor.

      Jane Puranananda

ALSO BY LAURI ROBERTSON

An Æsthetic of Stone
In Concert
Where Do the Memories Go?

In Loving Memory of Howard Blue (1959-2017)

As this 'inflection point in history'
suffuses the collective unconscious,
anything written after the beginning of 2020
must be called *Après*.

CONTENTS

I

II

I

I

THE YEAR OF SILENT CASTLES

Not that they were noisy to begin with.
How thin the air seemed.
No one knew we were here.
Did we tell anyone?
At least there was a 'we'.

The weather was lovely, truly
but wouldn't be for long
some of the loveliness itself
a harbinger—strange, warm wind.
Time was about to tell.

                    *

How hard we work
to make life peaceful
(peaceful the only
ethical choice now)
waiting for the next
fall. It will come.
It will.

                    *

The silence of Paris was deafening.
We were already deaf.

We had nothing to lose.
We were already lost.

The worker's faces darkly rimmed—
sorrow of ages, the masks of survival.

*

A life of small savor
looking at wisteria, abuzz
life in one's head, silly
but possible
avant.

*

I don't want to die.
I don't want to leave
even the fear.
I don't want to live
without you
but I want to live.

REFRAIN

The coffee is bitter, the chocolate is sweet.
Where to begin. Must we, over and over?
You don't even know what I'm talking about.

There are so many things:
Plague, war. War, plague. Plague upon plague.
No room for an inner life, or only such thing.

Everyone's flayed, everyone's lungs
are turned inside out. And yet, the world
the poor, troubled, undeserving world

seeps in, becomes the malleable dream
bellwether, whether or not, weather vane
open our veins, word salad, cacophony

absorbing a rhythm derailed
incoherent in every language
pain *doleur* pain.

                    *

The coffee is bitter, the chocolate is sweet.
We settled into a life unimagined, unimaginable.
What life is ever imaginable?

Smaller and smaller still, at peace with what
I would not call *deprivation*, but *sorrow*.

The cat is content. That I know almost certainly
enrobed in my love for as long as he shall live.
We'd each be unlucky if he outlives me.
I didn't know how unique they are.

(Do not further torture me by putting *very*
in front of *unique,* saying *unprecedented*
one more time, or guaranteeing a decade
of fucking Covid poems.)

                   *

The coffee is bitter, the chocolate is sweet.

What to make of this life. What to make
of it now, at this particular moment in time?
Why do we keep asking the same questions
over and over, with or without Kristallnacht?
The blood still crimson scarlet carmine.
Our neighbors then, and our neighbors now.

Each moment making the last look calm.

                   *

The coffee is bitter, the chocolate is sweet.
It's cloudy, and the sun is going down.
No, not a country western song
just a fact, a canticle. In fact
it's been cloudy for days. Do we mind?
It's a sacred cloudy time of year
confined until a real breath of real air
becomes necessary, or possible.

FOR TEN IN SALBRIS

"There are natural deaths as always in a nursing home,
he *nuances*."
    —The Mayor of Salbris
        (*via* Google Translate, emphasis mine)—

Maybe it was late, at night, too late
and they said, *Let's go, we are ready.*
Let's go now, not alone, but together.

Those who could not speak
blinked in unison their accord
serious, not quite solemn.
And those, like the 4th child
at a Passover Seder, who could not
understand, no longer understand
consented—their faces still washed
bellies still full—with gratitude.

It was very late.
We wanted to be young, and had been.
We wanted to be young again
but it was not possible.
We wanted to love, and loved
false or true.
We wanted to live, and did
the years prove.

Some said, I do not want to be left
waiting amidst the carnage
to save old bones for light years
instead of life years. Ration my skin
ration my memories, cherish or
weep that I was every born.

I am so ordinary.
I am so old.
I owned little.
I was proud of some.
I cooked for my family
and they ate happily.

THE SECRET GARDEN
—for George Floyd

Substance

Life passing before one's eyes, coming full circle.
Pile the bodies high... Shovel them under...

Turning the secret garden under, over and over.
Even this place of quiet contemplation explodes
into a song of blood, or hope.

Who has enjoyed their prosperity, dreamed
in America/Amérique/Amerika/Ameryka
and lived, by some, by others, and no longer?

The fruit of the vine has a bitter aftertaste.
Our cruelty to each other is impeccable.

Ghetto phoenix, with a wet-ink bill
3 illicit substances (depending where you live)
and, oh yeah, a rap sheet.

But, you were tall, and many people loved you.
I went to the funeral, I saw. They did not
make you up. No counterfeit.

   ...Who made him dead to rapture and despair,
   A thing that grieves not and that never hopes...

As if you were new to centuries.
New to whom?

   ...What dread hand? & what dread feet?//
   What the hammer? what the chain?

To this earth that turns, predictably
as the secret garden blooms.

Ghetto dweller, can you spare a smoke?
I gave it up years ago. White America
lives longer that way, and so many ways.

Who deserves to live longer?
Who's lucky enough to live at all
and weep with rage, for how long?

Thankfully

The cat killed a lizard this morning.
Thankfully, he didn't eat it. They're poisonous.
Thank goodness it wasn't a bird.
I'd have been shunned for not caging him.

I saw two yellow finches this morning and
warned them, told them to warn their families.
I saw a palatial 'catio' and well, imagine
living in a cage.

There's a kind of incoherence this morning
that goes with now, our virus spring-loaded
#BLM now, too upsetting for sense.
But, you get the idea, neither goodwill nor bad

any will at all, breath, contemplation, lyric
can undo lived, living history, no morning
is long enough to actually be now.
What does it mean to be 'contemporary'?

Any cigarette, bought or sold, is bad for you
anyway. And, they're never free.

Lola

Not that I don't understand
though it's hard to understand.
But, I mourn, a kind of professional mourner.
'Our Lady of Perpetual Mourning'.
Jews are good at it.

My friend Lola who, BTW is black
used to go to other people's funerals.
(Well, of course, not her own.)
But, not her people, just others, always in abundance.
Was it like *The Sin-eaters* eating the sins of the dead?

She never said. In all fairness, I never asked
or did, and she didn't say. Now, I need to know.
I want to join her every day, the return to the sky
the march of nature, *the grave you dig for me*
in honor, in remembrance, apology

incandescent, inevitable, *where*
no, *I* do not *long to be.*

Mama

I didn't think I could say more.
I didn't think I could say
anything at all.

The din of the world.
The espaliered apple tree
is absolutely huge

probably going to die soon.
They don't live forever.
But, the secret garden endures.

Oh, I just saw a heron
or egret, stork-like, flying
with incontrovertible distinction.

There's always more to say
but *never more*
never again.

"I want to touch the world." he said
as we all do, and do, briefly
9 minutes 29 seconds

of breath
silence
Mama.

Inflection Point

It's always been true
lives and lifetimes are punctuated
by the events of history.

Why should it be any different
now? Our decades framed
by failure, and catastrophic

foolishness, all kinds of bleeding
for each other, for nothing
but our own perverse natures.

I cannot find another way
to say this in 'a poem':
Millions unable to breathe

because of what we couldn't see
became one man unable to breathe
because of what we saw.

Water

Did we ever really think
about how he strode
how he fled, or how deeply
he felt, a large black man
among thousands of black men
trying to tap dance on water?

Woke

When I am safely here
my arms exhausted from rowing
the conflation of motive and time
too muddled to know
what to dread first.

Who is 'I'? Why are you speaking?
And, safely where? Where is 'here'?
The Secret Garden? Why are you 'rowing'?
Is there water? Troubled? What is
safety? How will you know?

Before, the light poems were tinged.
A good culture has arms of sorrow.
After, even the heavy ones
seem light and frivolous.
Avant—Après.

Please sir, you're killing him.
You bastard, you're killing him.
Murderer, you're killing him.
I didn't watch. I couldn't.

But, how I've dreamed
of having been there, and spoken
gestured and shrieked, as if
own body on the pyre.

Verdict

The secret garden, again.
It serves so many purposes—

to keep my husband from going mad
during the plague. To delight, and mourn.

Once beautifully, if not exquisitely cared for
now beyond shabby. Yes, it is.

The espaliered apples are on their knees.
Yes, an allegory. The gate is rusted, collapsing.

Weeds and brambles go without saying.
Yes, it's a ruin no one would want responsibility

for reviving. Like America, a world
beyond. We come here to love

all we've ever loved, to reach beyond
anything we've ever touched or seen

or to do nothing but sit among crazy vines
framed by the beautiful stone of our *centre ville*

also crumbling. I try to think, but pause on *lush*.
Here, toward the salient, the *tsuris*

of the world, this garden with its chest
filled with thorns without roses

trying so hard to be an articulate helicopter.
A few tulips, a tree peony still make it

without thinking of cruelty or loss
thinking only of the infinitesimal victory

that now we can believe our own eyes.

Beyond

People can cry much easier than they can change.
—James Baldwin

The earth is dry.
A long, thin arm pulls a weed from the thyme.
The hollyhocks are coming, and a white morning glory.
I do not know if it's an invasive imposter.
My strange husband likes the garden wildly unkempt.
It isn't his—we call it *the secret garden*—
he trespasses, and sits in the last light of day
growing into an old man.

It's beautiful, I have to say, beautifully designed
by someone who died, and shed to a relative.
I have to say, except for an absence of urgency
it's particularly lovely, and right, now.

We feel a great need to pierce the urgency.
Send their dogs to bite our bodies. Is there ever
there is never, a time without urgency.
Now I sit, growing old too, crying in waves.

Speak up, white woman. What will you say?
That you write poetry in an untended garden?
Is there something beyond the secret garden
beyond the color of tears?

Rage...

...is all the rage, the id unbound.
Black rage, white rage, international
permission to speak. We tried so hard
to be civil, civilized, for what?
It's time to speak.

For example, I'm nice but now I think
the only good Republican is a dead
Republican. Who did that to me?
Who wrecked my peace? Peaceful
old age? Nice, wry *Kumbaya?*

The rage of nations, no biblical hope
the language gets worse, even
nice upper-mid women curse, a lot.
The bristling rage, like caterpillar
or anchovy hairs, always upon you.

Did you know that *rage* in French
is *rabies?*

DEAR GOOD REPUBLICANS

(If there are any good Republicans...)

Come over to the light side.
The sweetest of snowflake, tree-hugger
United Nations echo chambers await you.

Fact is, I don't actually know any Rs
or not many, or have successfully forgotten.
How's that for tribalism? But, please come.

There's decency here, prosperous enough
to be concerned without cheesy American
theatricality, or frank psychosis.

Come over, the Ivy League awaits you
(not really), but surely you'll like science.
It's tried and true—no tetanus, smallpox, polio.

I've always thought about that day 50 years ago
on Wall Street, workers marching with flags
as bayonets. I ran as screams converged
and thought for half a century:

Something is wrong. These people are not my enemy.
These are people we're fighting for.

And, still are. Sometimes I think
the cataclysm is silly, like red and blue
football teams, or some other
dumb, testosterone-fueled sport.

The world is laughing at us
and crying for us.
Trust me
they are.

WHITE TO BLACK

Right and reason to be enraged
for four hundred years?
Are all successful black people supposed
to lose their black accents? Yes, we recognize

the intonation, like New Yorkers or Jews.
Or Southerners, about whom I know nothing.
Hispanic or Asian, Italian, Russian, German
Indian, *français*. So distinctive, Cockney.

Why did we all want to talk like Walter Cronkite
the nicest of dead white men, anyway?
I write with white guilt, of course—
Faulkner's line read half a century ago:

I thought of all the children coming forever and ever
into the world, white, with the black shadow
already falling upon them before they draw breath.

But, envy too, for a mostly real mother
to have raised me, not a 13 year old like
white trash, but someone like Toni Morrison.
(There's no one like Toni Morrison.)

But, maybe her mother, and father who
wouldn't let a white person in the house.
Those good and patient enough to
hold their heads high, quietly, quixotically

rageful enough to bow their heads
in those little storefront churches
I was bewildered by, hearing the music
too lonely to know the gift.

God and a ghetto church, if that's all
you have, is so much, and so much more.
I'm not begging for forgiveness.
I'm begging to belong.

                    *

Is a poem a dialogue? Or, a dialectic (whatever that means)?
Some kind of conversation, with the world or one's neighbor?
A listener, or none? Because no one listens these days.
I am an old woman. Not quaint, or retro, or delivered into
a universe re-invented even in a few short decades, trust me
they are short. What was radical then seems obvious now
but took a great deal of conviction to say. I doubt that we
humans, humane, just us, will change, much, but some.

#BLM
Who has said how bizarre and bitter the need
to say these words? I say to The Confederacy
say *goodbye*. Black women were good enough
to raise your children, to suckle and bathe them.
You swam in *their* Baptismal font. Let them
raise you now, your scarred, brutal bones
you who believed it was *normal*. Say *goodbye*
to everyone, including your white children
in a kind black world we all nursed from.

Mouzieys-Panens 2020
—for Toni Morrison

Solomon

Lavender, rosemary, honeysuckle
mint, sage, thyme, oregano, even
chive with its purple signifier.
Toni Morrison might forgive—

Instead of reading *Song of Solomon*
I've pressed all of these, every one
in the book, the pages stained
with ghostly chiaroscuro.

Fragrant beyond any escape
and in a world of love, still
if you're willing to respect solitude
not loneliness, we hope.

I came, much belatedly, with perfect
intention, but discovered raking instead
weeding reading weeding reading.
The scent overwhelming, the formation

of leaves enough to confound
a *Linnæan Herbarium*, all in accord—
mélange, electric bees in flight, offerings
sec ou frais, or burnt.

Forgiveness

Forgive me [   ] for I have sinned.
I'm an ethnic Jew with no religion, a poetry
from who knows where, I know nothing of.
The space is blank because I have no *Dieu*.

I loved my real, human father. No forgiveness
needed for gratitude. Forgive me [   ].
The space is blank because some unlocatable
undefinable pain lives only within the hollows.

I've been successful, but greedy, generous but needy.
I've done good things to feel good, and because I could.
I tended my own garden almost too carefully.
I've tended platitudes for lack, perhaps, of courage.

I've lived well, better than well, but with a nagging sorrow.
Should I try now, in old age, to escape again, or concede?
Is it my own? Forgive me [   ] for I've read WF
appreciated the Godless Jew, striven for legitimacy.

Forgive me for cultural appropriation.
The Mad Class doesn't have any culture of our own
beyond dream, apparition, exhausted muddled
longing, memoir, madness.

Forgive me, but there's a story I haven't told.
The mad mother got the sympathy. I had
to be nice, a girl, age 8, in a photograph
with dirty socks, hands on hips.

Ancestor

My *dear,* yes you are.
How everywhere you are
in song, in the clouds.
How incandescent your laughter.
How I cannot stretch meaning
to mean anything beyond
everything you say, and are.
I've crawled in and out
of your words until until until
they mean more than the sky
their incandescent hate buried
in laughter, their incandescent
love, my longing. They were
the color of flame, until you were
ash. Now, the color of eternity.

So Long Polite

So long polite. It's paralytic.
But, you had to be because
they were the ruling class.

No more in this post-post-
modern post-apocalyptic chaos.
No more bewildered survival.

You can't give someone a culture
but you can't take it away completely.
So long polite. It's paralytic.
The disenfranchised write poetry
because what else is there to do?
Because they can.

Stone walls do not a prison make
nor iron bars a cage.
(except when they do).

And, because some want to more
and more than anything else.
Toni Morrison was nonplussed

by the fancy publishing house.
"I was more interesting than they were."
She said, and was by light years.

Tell all the truth but don't *tell it*
slant anymore.

"Vingt-vingt"

As my American neighbor in France calls it
twenty-twenty—the year two thousand and twenty.
I was looking forward to a peaceful old age.
Tough shit, old woman.

I especially wasn't looking forward
to Covid poetry for the rest of my life
however long that may be, most probably
not long enough to see in the rear view mirror.

Those Chaplinesque walkie films of 1918?
War or plague, take your pick. The Great War
had to change its name. *Never Again?*
And, my country, like a ruined castle.

I'm trying to see, won't someone, an ultra-
prestidigitator help me buy a ticket now?
Just 20 minutes in 100 years? I want to see
am dying to see. Curiosity killed the cat.

Vingt-vingt. The year I read Toni Morrison
belatedly, *all* of Toni Morrison, without
stopping, except to cry. Belated, *Beloved.*
It's not the fault of the visionary.

If you're white and don't understand #BLM
just try being black for a minute or 2, a week
or a year, a lifetime in America if you're not
'exceptional', and cannot shed *the bit.*

1963—my friend's mother, dancing around
singing Joan Baez, Peter, Paul & Mary
a housewife in Queens with her own regrets—
But, we don't want to give them the country, do we?

Isn't it their country, already? I didn't say.
I was 10. But, I remember, more than
half a century later. Just try being
black in America. Just try being.

Vingt-vingt. The year democracy died
not in silence as the NYT says, but in plain
demagogic sight. We simply don't know how
to stop irrationality. It leaves us polite

pacifist, libtard, snowflakes stupefied.
What can you say to killing 100 years
of science instead of a virus?
Sorry, I hope you don't get sick...

I know there must be another side
but, for now, *fuck you vingt-vingt.*

WHAT MAKES YOU THINK

What makes you think
if there's a drop of water left
you should be the one to drink it?

Or, a life raft, a cure, a bed, or
a bath, a soldier of the liberation
an organ transplant?

What makes you think the roulette
wheel, or nonexistent God will favor?
Or thick skin, good will, or even desire?

Only half of London died in 1348
meaning, half lived. Half empty
half full, brief, no matter what.

I love my life so much (tho' not always)
my own, individual existence, so filled
with feeling, and love for the herd.

So few answers, as if there were
real questions. Celebrate with patience.
Kiss, bless, relinquish. I love you.

As a kid I had a little diary, and wrote
on the faux gilt edge, "I love humanity.
Does humanity love me?"

My father saw it and chuckled
bemused if not bewildered
or alarmed.

A STAND OF TREES

They are regal and kind, yes trees
can be kind. Fuck you if you don't like
nature poems at this moment in time.
They're natural, pastoral, pasture-all.
Fuck you if you don't like vulgarity.
The moment is vulgar beyond artifice
if you can't conceive of irony as sincerity
heartbreak, warriors as filled with love
copse, as if there were no enemies.
There are no enemies, just sorrow
anger and trouble. Who cradles whom?
It feels so new, but look at history if you
have eyes to look. Of course mere eyes
can't see what's been lost over centuries
lost again this century, this moment of time.
Fuck you for saying the word *unprecedented*
again and again and again and again.
The stand of trees is still here, majestic
and foggy all at once, common but
a beauty I can live with forever, for
the rest of my life, which is not forever.
Why don't I *know* more about *something*
the branches that curl like crazy smiles
a palette soft, as it should be. I think of
Adrienne, a fragment that comes, as all
fragments, all stands, all trees, all histories
and broken hearts, vulgarities, all natures
poems, all enemies, sorrows, cradles come:
Tenants that neither speak nor stir
Yet dwell in mute insistence.

I Hear That Those Who Cannot…

I that those who cannot walk
dream of running, in great sinewy strides
their muscles taut as the shoulder of a horse
rippling with desire.

I am merely aging, each step becoming cautious
a warning, a languid stretch will suffice.
Or, I am old, each perhaps, a shuffle, a slide
swimming into cataclysmic oblivion.

I hear that those who cannot swim
drown, over and over, their hair like seaweed
their tears the oceans, their mouths open
as if singing without remorse.

I hear that those who cannot sing
imagine a heavenly choir, The Met perhaps
as if birds and whales are their voices
arcing into the strangest of places.

I hear that those who cannot sing
cherish the silence. …who cannot speak
moan in basements and cages
while we skip breakfast, while it is said

They speak a vision of their own heart

and they pray, because even if it's just
a metaphor, all animals know how.
I hear that those who cannot breathe
die.

INAUGURAL

Birth placed me here
not elsewhere
across the continents

or in the body
of an animal
instead of a little girl

a saucer-eyed
orphan of drought.

An accident of birth
on a planet now small
enough to hear whispers.

A fortunate accident.
The water is mostly pure.

Where truth comes
in orders of magnitude:

Someone thought they
were born on a flat earth
but over and over, truth

said *No.*

A fleet of rainbow coats
means so many things, is
beautiful, and makes us sing!

A wise old man is good.
Why isn't it that simple?

SPRING

I've never liked spring so much
just in the air, flowers sure, *fleurs*
just a few so far, the daffy daffs, jonquil
jonquille. (Oh, don't go poetic on me.)

A bit of cheery forsythia, lilac portent
but, I have never liked the air so much
not even warm, some nights dipping into
tundra, the embalming crust once comforting
but the air itself, twitchy as the animals.
(A fat rabbit came across the stone plaza
to our front door the other day.)

Twitchy! No *For what purpose, April, do you return*
or *cruelest month.* I love the vesting of remorse—
it's barely March. I've loved being unable
to dance, grousing at abdication of gravity
(gravitas). But, this year, abandon all
grievances, spring is as if birth, life, renewal
fresh, fresh, fresh (don't you hate redundancy?)
air!

In Concert Après

Masked

Wait for the moment, the magic
as if a drug. Is there still music *après?*

There are still notes and instruments:
what a tree and gut, the tail of a horse
can become and remain even now, *après.*
Even after forests have burned.

Baroque few know: Matteis and Locke
Finger, Banister, strangely compatible names
now we know, vibrating through centuries.

A strange instrument, too, like a giant lute
a crazy, aberrant vegetable in the squash patch:
théorbe—the globe—music of burning Romes
and drowning Titanics. *Le monde Après* goes on.

Courtly and sweet, the youthful (of course)
musicians smile, a harp tilts, the harpsichord
already horizontal (of course), a guitar rotates in.

The notes are happier than the young bones
playing them, the masked audience, elderly
(of course) trying to return to life, *après.*

With great feeling somewhere, we all seem
strangely remote, dissociated this *après.*
Let something, however slowly, filter back.
Nice summer casual, fresh effort, even kindness
a nod, a smile, seem shrunken and small.

We are living *après*, bunches of inverted hearts
of white hydrangea on stage bursting forth.

It is lovely. I am unmoved. It is too lovely
après. Not even a shard of irony saves it
just the hint of sorrow, spritely hearts
trying to beat *après*.

Bach & Shubert

Too cheerful, too spritely these, chirping
for a long dead court. The 1st violin jiggles and bobs
her blood red dress in layers visible down to the lace.
But, what's wrong with courtly cheer, mannered

and decorous? Their moment of plague no better
than ours. The hydrangea have lasted or been refreshed.
They really are like inverted hearts, ghostly white
as if their blood already drained, already heavenly.

We have a new friend who recites poetry:
Eliot and Frost, Yeats. Heaney, maybe.
(Why is this comment here? Except that
they all commented so well, for so long.)

So many lives, regard them all. So many
different lives, each plaintively, inescapably
their own. Some like poetry and some
like cheer, the abrogated music of poetry.

Now, not sad but more serious, an awareness
of storms, and guillotines. Something Germanic?
The 1st violin is still bobbing, but now plunging
and weaving, the red more essential, less decorative.

She knows now life can be threatened. Her violin
can warn and bray. Cellos cry even when singing.
Now softly, not quite tears, but cheer in abeyance
stroked and listened to in this year of life *après*.

II

II

TRIBAL

Do you crack the nut with your hand
your teeth or a tool? What custom

tradition is cherishable to you?
Or will be when it's almost

all you can remember, the ritual
of the family perhaps that bore you.

Everyone, absolutely everyone
has to come from somewhere.

When her son was born the adopted woman said
"He's the first person I've met who's related to me."

Must there always be blood belonging?
What if the seed is no good?

What if 'necessity' and 'loneliness'
however ancient, aren't what they seem?

What if there are no answers and the questions
themselves long and unworthy?

There's truth before you that fades like a kiss
carved from a mouth or a mountain.

It's raining this morning. The clouds
are like mountains, a soft mouse gray blue

with that other nimbus breaking through.

Po-em

Once upon a time we
learned it has two syllables
and felt smart, smarter than
the other kids who said
pome. After all, we were
the smart class. You can't say
it was about *class* though. We
were all middle class back then
or so we thought. The first time
I walked past Bergdorf's
after riding the subway
for a dime, holding onto
a cousin's hand, and also
saw the skating rink, I didn't
get it. I just didn't get it.
Now, I think *pomme,* an apple
in France. Now I think
an apple is just as good
as a poem, just different. Why
should one thing be better
than another? One street
one life, one pronunciation
differentiation, syllable, verse
fruit, labor? Why do we strive
for one-up emptiness?
They told us early we were
smart. It was instrumental.

COOKBOOK

"If my South Indian father hadn't found himself in a Kan-
sas wheat field thirty years ago, this book would
never have been written."   —Maya Kaimal

Why do these words bring
tears to my eyes? They are, after all
only an introduction to a cookbook

and, best I can tell, the interesting
prosperous family fared entirely
well. But, it's a time of immigrants

of soothing skins, even 3rd generation
Ellis Islanders who never looked back
or thought there was anything

to look back to. That was them
and we are now. A time of reckoning
or not, of recipes? Your grandmother's

and mine, even unremembered, made
up, or a just decorative plate. Who made
up 'authenticity', weeps from nostalgia?

If *there's nothing left now but the food
and the humor,* is that enough? More
than enough? My spice to blend

with yours, or radically distinct? This is
no metaphor. This is how we love, those
of us who are lucky enough to eat.

If I am in France, do I want to be
somewhere *French,* with French bread
and French fries and everything else

Americans slobber over?
If I am black in America do I
have my own country anywhere?

If I am old and trying to remember
do I have my own words
for sustenance or flavor?

If I had no mother, if I gave up
envy, fled to safety, if my creaturehood
is limpid, do I have my own right
to hate those who are hateful?

THE ISLAND

The rich play with the poor
sort of, or more, but believe me
there's rare mistaking
who is whom.

The artists I feared
might devour each other
are actually the nicest because
they have something to do.

The government is your friends
and neighbors. Incompetence
comes home. I learned how truly
unable to rule we are.

But, there's lots of fun, and oysters, too!

People doing stuff
they never could have done
jobs they never could have held
in 'the real world'.

Characters, lots, characters
v'chetzy, even a few Jews now
at the Yacht Club.
The Yacht Club.

A ghetto of wealth, salvation
was half a dozen half a century ago
saying *No*, preserving half
in perpetuity.

We moved here
renegades for beauty
weathered board and flora.
The sea, ubiquitous, came with.

The first thing I did was
go to the cemetery. It was
comforting to know actual people
had lived and died here.

What I Wish I'd Studied

Don't know much about history
and that's the sad truth. Thought
it was about memorizing the date
of the Louisiana Purchase.

Our 5th grade classmate who excelled
became an accountant. Didn't know
that history told and untold, woven
or spun, was, and is, us.

And, forget music, don't know
a sonata from a cantata. Ok
I do know a flute from a lute.
But, the real lacuna is economics

and I don't mean Home Ec. How
can you 'borrow' from the future?
A so-called future that isn't even here yet?
Whom are we borrowing from, Martians?

And, if such a thing is possible, why not
just keep doin' it and doin' it 4ever?
Give everyone everywhere something
enough, including birth control.

The Classics are the saddest of all
Ain't got no classics, or class. Can't
keep the names or the centuries
straight. Greek to me. How many

used copies of Edith Hamilton
can one buy before giving up?
Have you ever seen the family tree?
They invented us. Reinvent us, please.

House Philosophy
—for those lucky enough to have a place to live

You don't need many rooms
just one or two, to sit in, like a dog
who's circled and circled and found
and live in, imagine it's home.

You need a serviceable kitchen—
not fancy, that helps not worrying
about messing it up—unless
you don't like to cook.

And, if you have to have a
goddess-damn garden make it
small! You need a place to sleep
which can be anywhere dreams are.

You need a view, or one
an *inward eye* can see.
You need a roof, if I forgot
to say, and a key, if necessary.

But, what you need most
is perfection, a place you
imprint upon, the *ahhhh*
and, of course, modesty.

Let Us Now Praise...

—for Lucille Boroughs

On my wall
a gift for my 18th birthday
from the boy I lost my virginity to:

A Walker Evans' Library of Congress print.
How famous. For years I've been asked
if it's me, though so obviously not.
Though I sought some truth
that can only be found in poverty
stripped of every inclination.

How sad the need to be heroic
just to survive, that escaping
however beautifully done
is the only striving. I'd say
there's no reaching for the sublime
except we can't help reaching.

For years I didn't know
about her life, or death.
Who can imagine her life?
A reservoir for sorrow?
Who knew it would go that way?
Or, for any of us?

Suddenly, I feel luckier than
the stars, not otherwise benighted.
It could have been otherwise.
Could it have been otherwise?
If the camera had given more
than taken a graven image

another life entirely, a train ticket.

How Tired

—What is poetry which does not save /Nations or people?

How tired we get of stories
especially someone else's
especially our own—
desecration, destruction, damnation—
though keep searching for the one
the meta-story that will *tell*
all the truth without rowing weary
grand grandstand small tale.
How stupidly they tug
at our humanity. How belatedly
a line of Milosz makes me weep.

LONELY HEARTS

All that strange sorrow
and ordinary sorrow
its strange repetition.

Not the lover you miss
but the having been loved.

Those you write of are dross
unworthy figments, but not them.

Some even try to warn:
I'm not your lover
I'm the fantasy of your lover.

And so, the schmuck is correct.
You are not able
to be kind to yourself.

Loneliness is not a punishment
for being unlovable.

We exchange our mortal wisdom
and platitudes, voices conversant
with each other's plights.

Once I insisted that he'd bought
the earrings I bought for myself.

PRAISE

Don't expect more
than you can give yourself.
Or, an abundance of other babble
if you've curried, or deserved
will mean nothing, ephemeral
as an ice cream cone, or worse
anathema.

Treat yourself, or at least say
it's allowed, once in a while.

But remember, when you're
most deprived, others are
parched beyond survival, too
and that strange sometimes truth:
It's better to give than to receive.

ADMONITION

You know, we have what we have.
We don't have what we
don't have, and never will.

This goes for friends and lovers
parents, partners, children, and pets.
Love them each, each one

in heart and palm and memory
as they are, no more. As you
meld as you imagined them

with as they are, your vision changes
your need for them to be. *To be
or not to be* is not a question
but an illusion.

And, there are chapters.
Find the right time, métier
context, snack, moment
of tenderness, a story that is not

abstract. I want to be your friend.
Take me as I am, and I will
take you as you are, and try
in all modesty to be

whom you want me to be.

BESTOW

– for JV

If you cannot go to the sea
the sea will come to you
with extraordinary purpose
and bring you
extraordinary purpose
the mother before
the daughter after
sisters above and below
they are here to tell you
how it is done.
Part of the answer is *softly*.

DIET

The body says
the body does.

Sometimes I can
and sometimes I can't.

The scourge
or revolt.

Still you know, you
want want want

to be lovely
in a particular way

to eat
like a stray cat.

The body says
and does.

Arts & Letters

Well, I've got letters
too many—*more degrees*
than a thermometer—
dancing in my head.

Where does it get you?
To the upper-middle class
a striving for which I now
hold in complex contempt

or that it was not least
for revenge. No regret but
for a culture more degradation
product than else, over-fed
and starved at once.

It's as possible as it is
impossible to know yourself
by reciting your letters.

*

I know you don't believe
in prizes. Prizes for all.
Or the faux of celebrity.
But, what about arrivals?
Simply coming to the door
with one's wares, placing oneself
in a landscape familiar as home.

Perhaps home for the first time.

ANOREXIC

It wasn't my not weighing anything
So much as my not knowing anything.—
— Robert Frost, "Wild Grapes"

Not about the body, the absence
of a body, a bodiless crime.

I speak as someone who never could be.
I am the opposite. I gobble infinity.

Still, I admire them, not for suffering
certainly not death, but for building mountains

to reach the stars, an ascetism pure enough
to inhale the bones of saints.

Mortification cum vivre.

Large and loud, I try to make the earth flat
graze down to the nub, to walk without falling

sleep without sliding, kiss without regret.
My argument is with a world

that deprived me, made me a stray
not let me taste all the crazy fruit at once.

Not even about hunger, just a mouth
open for bounty—Helen Keller grabbing

scrambled eggs in her palm
every morsel from every plate.

Their argument is within armored walls
of delicate skin, hunger's razor swaged/assuaged.

Hungrier than I know, I know.

Our methods are different but, perhaps
oddly twinned. Satiety eludes us.

Some things can be cured in the body
but not the mind.

We want to devour the world
but it doesn't fit.

DEAR SARA,

I've scanned some old negatives from
1975, including this one. The women
may have been your roommates that
semester you spent at Oxford. (Yes,
The Oxford!) I wonder if you recognize
them, a very pretty young woman with
red hair, though you cannot tell from
a black and white photograph. But
maybe you can, something distinctive
about gingers. No freckles, though.
Why did we care so much about being
pretty, good old feminists that we were
in the good old 70's? Do we still care?
She really is lovely. The other girl-woman
is cute, too. Youth alone is beautiful, so
fresh. She's lying at the edge of the image
not 'edgy', but kind of contemporary
this half a century later, or vintage or
retro, nouveau. What's become of them?
Do you know? Have they had good lives?
What's a good life anyway? Love and luck
and generosity. Longevity we now say
Yes, yes, please to with fresh gratitude.
Were they famous or happy, rich or rich
enough, buried by tragedy? Has her beautiful
black and white-rendered red hair turned
gray? Did she love or create? Create
children or art, or dinners or days?
Did she age? Of course she aged! Has she
aged out of life, yet? And, but, dear
Sara, what about you, whom I haven't
spoken to in almost as many years? You
the weaver who liked to dance. What about
time passing, having passed? Are you

still alive? Memory is as acute as day.
What are you doing or have done with
this, as they say, *one life,* we're given?
More than one person has asked
Why don't you put words with your photos
photos with your words? I say, *No*
(and learned the word 'ekphrastic')
I don't think they go. But, here's another
answer. (Isn't there always another?):
A photograph to prove the words, perhaps
speak the truth. In color though, please!
Let the beautiful red-haired young
woman be in color before she fades.

TRAUMA

The legacy of trauma is a veil
of unreality, or only one's reality.
I can live lonely, and did for a long time.
It swathed me, a sack cloth.

I cannot live unquiet though, *inquiétude*
French for worry, only. There has to be
some kind of peace, breakfast out
in a shabby café. A river, or a dream

of a river. I remember a psychotic man
with long gray hair, family-less
an androgenous name, he explained
being both. I understand now, belatedly.

They chain-smoked "to get the talk off"
rocked because toes had been lost to frostbite.
Rocked more from the meds. But the delight
of sitting along the Charles with a "teeny little

sandwich", they said, nicotine-stained
fingers curled in a gesture of holding it.
One can have dread, but not only.
One needs musing, silliness and morsels.

Delight of saying, creating nothing.
Delight even of being homeless
until the toes froze. I understood
even envied them. Maybe it was hope.

III

MANTLEPIECE

There is only this: the photograph
of woods in Brittany, wild
and dense, almost atonal
that I adore, more and more
every year.

And the little Persian silver vase
you carried home long before
it was home. Pierced brass candle holders.
Nothing 'rich', just what we see
every day, some days almost all day.

There's a postcard of a rabbit
barely visible in its milieu of camouflage.
I am at peace here, improbably
wanting to see as little as possible
for a forever that does not exist.

A piece of pottery, too, by a new friend.
A small carpet to call us
to atheist prayer, the andirons
one you polished with vigor
then gave up. You

so near, I cannot see you
so known I cannot know you
as other, strange as you are.
We found decades though
I speak my disbelief.

We found homes, or forged them
out of wood and history, now
stone, where our eccentricities
love each other
as we do.

Impossible to tell you to be still
to continue only to cherish the forest
the actual happiness, true happiness
density of breath created
over and over.

Marriage, cont'd

"I don't want to be infantilized."
"What's the difference between
infantilized and *waited on?*"
"I'll *allow* you to consider," he said.

Leaving *that* alone, after decades I know
there are some things he cannot do.

Even if he empties the drain
after pleas, if not provocations
animations, he will never clean
its darkening rim, nor the sink itself
the silting puddle under the cutting board.

This man, who can specify
1,400 pieces of stone for a castle
sketch, freehand, placement of 500 tiles.

Am I married to the wrong person?

I cook, year after year. OK, well
I like to, with a fearless, hurried flair
(though afraid of most everything else).
More to the point, I don't really
want to eat his fare.

MARRIAGE, CONT'D #2

They don't call it a relationship
for nothing, i.e., related ships

sometimes at sea. We're going
to have dinner on the balcony.

Carry the stuff up. That part
of effort disappears, becomes

normal, *ahhh,* nor-mal... Sometimes
we forget, squabble like squirrels

complain like birds, conjoint twins
who ignore each other completely.

Once, all I wanted was to sleep
close enough to dream far away.

GRATEFUL

Grateful not to be one
solitary, suspended
interlocutorless, that most
painful utterance, *lonely*.

Grateful you admit you're
impossible, and grateful
you put up with me.

Grateful war is usually slight:
you bought me a croissant
and when I came down
you'd eaten it. Ok, it was
two days later, but still, *'til
death are we considerate.*

Grateful it's easy
without effort or learning
each uneducable as we are.

Grateful for parallel play
your strange, obscure
expertise, centuries of history
roughhewn speculation
impracticalities, inattentions
socks in the fruit bowl
dreams that come true.

OLDER COUPLES

Older couples start to worry about
who will die 1st. Yes, we do, and
ponder actuarial assumptions.

Years ago I asked, "What would you do
if I died?" "You can't die." he said
"What would I eat for dinner?"

So now when I'm terrified of those
terrible tables, or an annoyed *hausfrau*
I say it declaratively: "I'm dying 1st."

Statistics don't know everything.
They don't even apply to individuals.
Sometimes it goes backwards

or upside down. Sometimes
it's cancer, usually, or jaywalking, a
ski accident, aneurysm, embolism.

So, for all my rumination
and threats, dread of certainty
it's not impossible I may actually be

dying 1st, unexpectedly, the cards
refuse to reveal, entirely without
anything that might be called bravery.

It will be quiet.
It will be silent.
It will be.

BIRTHDAY POEMS

You wouldn't be so mean
as to do me the disaster
of dying on my birthday.

But, I have to go upstairs to check.
We're sleeping apart because, well
old folks get restless, and old folks
really need to sleep, or try.

You were perfectly alive
though neither of us had made it
entirely somnolent through the night.

I'm gloomy today (said with a wink)
because it's my birthday.
Such things embarrass me
and almost worse, I'm almost seventy.

*

A dream my husband told me:
a house he built was crumbling
like skim coats over rubble in France.
The trees were pollarded, like in France.

"You're mixing up your continents." I say.
"Nothing lasts forever," he says.
"Not even stone." I reply. Not even stone
though it takes a long time...

Different as we are, we share rather profoundly
a love of old things, wanting to preserve them—
all of France, which preserves itself, sort of.
Antiquity laid bare.

Those chairs in the basement on another continent
you'll probably never see again, much less sit in.
I know you love the carving on the slats.
I thought in a flash to find a woodcarver.

But, some value in giving up all the preserving
lovely as it is, that's only about loss anyway
a great relief and lightening, quest not for the finest
chisel and awl, but to *let evening come*

as our friend Tom quoted.

SAFETY

You're safer in the air than on the ground
my father used to say, referring to
those afraid to fly. But, not always.

Think of the boat my husband brought home—
goddess lines to those in the know
a lovely wreck. He bought a hoop shed

and stuck it in a friend's yard.
There were long hours, and there was glee.
You have to wait for no wind to blow

dust on the varnish, you have to strain
said varnish. There were accoutrements.
Eventually he sold it to the new tenant.

I doubt the friend is still a friend
but I was happy—all those silly memes
why women live longer than men...

You're safer on ground than in the sea.

The Architect & the Psychoanalyst

He loves the future
more than anything, his days filled
with the ecstasy of prescience.

He likes to build things.
The buildings are never finished.
But, even abandoned, they

continue to grow in splendor.
He happens to be married
to a psychoanalyst. She loves

the past. Who knows why.
She wants to salvage ruins
or leave them to be

mourned eternally, a phoenix
rising not out of ashes but
of the ashes themselves.

Her days are filled with trolling
for the right word to make peace.
She cures by telling you

you can't have your every wish.
He cures by telling you
you can.

I Want the World...

...to be perfect
the train windows clean
clear, unclouded, every train
every window, everywhere.

I want death
to stop, unnecessary and
necessary death, the wisdom
of the agèd, trees and light

in paradise, or viewed
through insensate eyes. I want
perfection of the moment
the right amount of salt

in the soup, and of the future.
There's always the future
hope, and time for reparation
for perfection.

My husband says
The problem with growing old
is there's no future in it.

ALREADY LIVING

> *for* my husband who thinks a *pied à terre*
> in Paris will make him happy

We're already living
the good life.

Gooder than good.
I'm sorry if you're

melancholy.
Get a life, a good one

as the saying goes.
Change your life.

Or, unassailable, constitutional.
Whose was never meant to be?

The poor, the lonely
the mentally ill?

Get a good life if you can
figure out what that means.

I can tell you
what it does not.

VEUVE

When I am a widow
as I may well be
statistically, a cat

will not make me
happy, but entertain
with a kind of camaraderie.

A pottery class has
been on the list for quite
a while. I know exactly

what I want to do. Don't
try to teach me, just give me
glaze and kiln. I'll become

as a widowed friend said
as I was before you existed
salvage a self thought

no longer extant. Ha!
When have either of us
failed to exist? Our days

are gifts of freedom
to exist, our nights in which
we sleep close enough

to dream far away. Stay
only as close as you are
invisible, indivisible.

When I am not a widow
ever, because I'd rather die
than live without you...

OCD

As if I could save your life
with vigilance, and failing
to worry would kill you.

I know time simply doesn't
retreat. Each day is another
without promises.

Let the drum beat of worry
inquiétude, tell me tell me tell me
I love.

COMING OF AGING

Do you want to consider reality
therapy for how much energy
you really have, a day or sequence
of days, *stamina* as they say.

How shocking the decrement
especially for energizer bunnies
those filled with love—breath—
and lust for the universe.

Now, it's time to rest.
Unfailingly sad, as we wail
or accommodate, or rail.
The wisdom and the fury of being

old. The platitudes. Some do it better
than others through no fault
of their own. Not Erikson's *integrity*
vs. *despair*, exactly, but great truths

to be told, the privileges of having
lived, and living, but aching.
Healthy as a horse, as they say.
At the very least, a thumb hurts.

However Interesting

—for Margaret, Phil, Tom, Gene, Don, Linda, John, & Dick

However interesting, accomplished
celebrated you may be, let us fail

to weep for you at ninety. Why not
simply applaud that sorrow isn't warranted?

Is there ever a time sorrow isn't warranted ?
All the beloved quietly line up

and are given up. It's almost as if they're
still in the neighborhood, memory as good

as animate flesh, all the more so
when the balance tips. I can name them all

still, around one block, still, I think.
We know who must be next

or image we do—always surprises—but
sometime soon anyway, before too long

inevitably. Or, spectacularly, Susie at
one hundred and five. How soon is too soon?

It's not that we're sad just about them.
We're sad because we're sad.

We like to be sad. It has tooth
and resonance. We're never sad too soon.

SHABBY

Shabby, but not desolate, no.
Consoling in its antiquity, longevity.
The weather comes and goes in minutes
like moods, or creating moods.

Create me! The bay tree on the balcony died.
I forgot to water it the one hot week
of a cold spring. All its leaves are now
the color of terracotta, matching the roof tiles.

A spare year with spartan intention.
The mint, even mint was anemic, the dill
from seed gone to seed. Well, start over!
Subsequents, like youthful dreams

don't stay true, even if not poisonous
though some are, cucurbits for example.
Even cucumber! Who knew? Don't eat
the reincarnated Halloween pumpkin

left in the yard last year. Accept a few
cilantro nascents that refused to feather
a gifted pepper plant, unproductive but
leafy and proud, as a sign of life.

Lots

Lots of lessons
here. Don't
do it
when you're
too old
to do it.

Performing
to show you
can, or think
you can,
doesn't look
good.

It looks bad
or worse.
And, that's
the truth
for all of us.
So, if I think

I can still
cook dinner
maybe I can
maybe I can't
but don't
expect much

or me
to know
the difference.

Paresthesias

Like being dusted by a feather.
(Who, at this point, knows
what a feather duster is?)

Sensory ghosts, communicating
what, if anything? I am old and have
no way to communicate. Please

someone teach me hip-hop language
and cryptocurrency, a short-cut
to youth. Help me absorb

new decades, a new century.
I'm no Miniver Cheevy. I want
to stop complaining, understand

to feel something other than
random, ominous messages
through my skin.

Old Woman's Body

It's an insult I tell you!

Spider veins like tributaries of The
Amazon, Ohio and Monongahela
in Subcarpathian mountains.

Sags like that substitute teacher
who shouldn't have gone sleeveless.

Toenails rippled as horn. The yellow crusts
and scales have no daughter to smear them
with cream. One becomes reptilian. Why
should aging de-recapitulate ontogeny?

The face, well, that's simply a matter
of light. Try faded light (and fading eyesight).
There's peculiar revenge in watching
the beautiful catch up with the plain.
We (the latter) have grown into our mirrors
while you (the former) grow out of yours.

Exercise is neither for pleasure nor vanity
or even health, but just to keep moving.

Don't bite anything but gruel.

...don't miss the limb fur much, or pits
but the thinning pubis shocks the husband.
What did he expect, and where is *his* mirror?

The torso moves toward a profile
of the elderly Eleanor Roosevelt
bosom worthy of a brooch
proceeding one into the room.

Belly, well they say it's about cortisol.
You'll want the few extra pounds
when a wasting illness comes.

Thumb, apparently the most vulnerable.
Don't touch the touchpad too much.

Neck, don't get me started. And, take
your hippy skirts up (if you still have any)
now dragging for loss of inches.

Anything else? Spots? Dark spots
on light, white spots on top.
Liver and lichen, solar lentigo.
As it is said, we are all turning
to parchment.

Bunions befitting Paul Bunyan.

Oh, and *what, what?* What did you say?
Floaters and shade. Far lights tremble—
only one eye though. At least it's not
a brain tumor (we hope).

But, on the subject of the brain…
let me refrain.

And, please don't use the word *gnarled*
unless you're a really bad poet
or describing a tree.

I am not a tree, although sometimes
I wish I were a tree.

They live longer.
They stand taller.
They have birds in their hair.

DEMENTIA

The scent here
is so strong. It could be linden
but think gardenia, or jasmine.
Intoxicating.

I wonder if I'm being drugged
or hallucinating. It's lovely
in moments, unto nausea.
How quickly can things change.

We know they can.
From life to death, a mood, a cloud
the gentle animal without a shred
of warning. A song into a wail.

And, now these thoughts
are paired with the crushing fragrance
tears someday for what cannot be
remembered.

...*something in me understands /the voice...*

I do not want to continue
the lines of this love poem.
It's cadence that stays
in the language-borne brain

memory without knowing
what is remembered
the dancer with dementia
rising like a swan.

MAKING

A day too lovely to tell—
the high clouds making
the light make everything

silvery.

It's a simplification
but not, a yearning
but not.

A strange desire to make
words better, pictures
to want in view forever.

To work in clay, imprinting
feathers and fossils, to make
a vessel to hold something.

A rhyton.

It all evolves, restless and weary.
Who knew satiety makes
its own stellate octopus hunger?

AND, SO YOUR CHILDREN

And, so your children
will care for you
wearily, or not, of course
wearily. Or not, of course
if there are no children.

Don't let words play
they're children.

Children or not, now is
the only sloshing time.
Save your pennies for the care
no one really wants to render.

Ethics, mere morality, and a job
a shitty job. Forgive the lack
of metaphor.

Let words play, they're children.

What is there really
to look forward to? Real
estate? My husband spent our life
savings on the garage next door
and a garden the size of Eden
lest we're allowed to begin again.
Fortunately, it's hidden, so as it
goes to seed, sea, no one will see.

Now, about those children…

SWEATER

I am wearing a dead man's sweater
a nice man I didn't know well
who'd been living in a cottage
I was cleaning.

It was among his belongings
the next of kin didn't want—
his sister, and his lover
neither wanted much:

La Rochère goblets with bees
a sculpture of a monkey, I forget
what else. A lot went to TIOLI
Take It Or Leave It, at the dump.

It hadn't happened here
so death didn't feel very close
but overseas, a while before
and he'd been ill. Not all that old

but not lucky. I kept the sweater
because it's nice—white cashmere
with sort of raglan sleeves.
It fits me. When I wear it

I feel, I don't know what
not tumult, but something
persistent, every time I put it on
a dead man's sweater.

You can't steal from the dead
not really, or not at all.
I'd asked very carefully. No
no one wanted it.

I washed it by hand. No
it isn't creepy, or a memorial
but something I can't describe
not with words, anyway.

Why should language have
the power to create or destroy
bewilderment? What is it
about a dead man's sweater?

I don't know, so I wear it anyway.

The Missing Button

It didn't just get loose and fall off.
Let me tell you how it happened:
I took the sweater off to whack a fly.
The button shattered (and the fly lived).
At least the window is still intact.

I thought about replacing it
with one from the bottom or top
or another, similar, or different
perhaps ornamental. I thought
let the poor sweater be, let it
be incomplete, bespeak shabby
as if intent, weary of materialism.

I thought maybe not, I'm weary.
It's an old sweater, and I'm old.
I thought the glaring imperfection
may be more of a problem than I realize.
I thought, *I hate allegory.*

MEDICAL APPOINTMENT

This is God's railroad car
the God you don't believe in.
What direction did you
think you were going?
Like the car behind you
with coal about to be burned.
An avalanche of news
thundering along the track.
No news, nothing is new
Why do you want to know
what your already know?
The luminescence rattles
and heaves.

IV

THE CAT WENT OUT

The cat went out before breakfast
as is often the case.
When I called him a bit later
for that fragrant can of trout amalgam
he did not come. I called and called
and no cat came. No worry, spring
is intimating, so the animals
are all twitchy. So are the humans.

I turned and looked the other way
and saw, no, not *three islands in a bay*

but a rabbit! A bunny larger
than the missing cat, honey brown
with a little white ruff. The darling let me
talk, sweetly, did not flee, hopped
slowly toward the house. Perhaps
I could have touched the fluff, but
why have you transformed? What's
the purpose of a cat becoming a rabbit?

To what purpose, April, do you return again?

From predator to prey, would you run
if you had not become? Perhaps
I'm in need of a new love for a new
season. Something magical or wacky
something in which to search for meaning
that isn't there, as if imagination itself
was meaning. Come here, I love
your fur, beware, a wild animal may

carry illness without a trace. But
I want you to surround and laugh
with me, be a spirit who will never
need to cry, not even once.
Once upon a time a hedgehog came
to my same door. They, I've heard
will share in a bowl of cat food
alongside the cats. My new friend

will eat only grass.

THE UNIFANGER

No, he didn't bomb anyone. Nor
for that matter, bite.

He's just my cat
who one day yawned and revealed
his left front fang
was missing.

Symmetry erased!
Though it seemed without pain.

Where is your tooth
your big fat long spikey
front tooth?

That enameled needle
shorn at the root.
Why?

Now obelisk.
Transition.
Unicorn.

A metaphor for nothing.

No, the Cat Is Not,,,

...a metaphor
for anything. He, she
they just appear
in doorways and on
window sills (their specialty).
Placid until you trespass
transgress, even unknowingly.
Then, they flee, usually (while
I'm begging them to love me.)

Sometimes they make
'smiley eyes' or suddenly
need to groom, a fine
displacement (for all of us).

No metaphor
just company without
much labor, just a dish
of food, and water. Shelter helps.
All that most of us need
if we're lucky enough to find
for a start.

And affection on one's own terms
in exchange for loyalty
whatever that may be.

STRAY

He was an orphan, and I a stranger.
Let us be an interspecies family.
Kin comes out of a tin, or imagination
fortune, fortune cookie, or choice.
Where do I belong dear turtle with a shell
a home anywhere, at least metaphorically.
Does that count as enough? Invented?
Or, I am content because there's food
and water, a bed, a lover, a language
kin you have to search for and beseech
a world in which to live without dread
even of death, acceptance, truisms and
Hallmark sentiments (if there are any left)
whatever peace that can be found
or made.

Grateful Cat

I am grateful to have a grateful cat.
Not like the one who, when I returned
after a few days away, vanished in turn.

One who ignored me worse than a bureaucracy.

Or, one I read about on a favorite cat page
who scratched and bit their human friend
for months on end.

Charlemagne (Charlie) is grateful.
He's the only cat I've ever known
who expresses gratitude.

Small in stature, personality too if I must say
pleasantly redundant, decorous but sassy
(he's still a cat), smart though not a genius
impish, a little like Charlie Chaplin.

But, he's grateful. Somehow
he expresses gratitude, as in those early days
when he was ill and all he could do
was curl. He started to groom for the 1st time

in my arms. When I go away
he eats everything our nice neighbor gives him.
(I tell her to be generous, and he gets fat!)
He knows what it was like to be a stray.

How does one choose between food and affection?

When I return, and he hears my voice
he yowls with delight, forgiveness, or relief?
And he curls closer than ever, purrs
like a Jaguar F-Type R.

I'm grateful he tolerates me grabbing
and squeezing him, reciting the process
in a ridiculous whining tone along the way.

Cyclops Cat in Six Riffs
—with apology to Mary Oliver

There's no place for the lack of horror.
It was neither theater nor literature.
There was nothing to be learned.
The kitten was a Cyclops, as in mythology
and dead because, I guess, they cannot be.
I didn't know how to cry for such a thing
and yet I cried, far more for life than death.

*

My little one-eyed monster, no
not an eye lost to battle or infection
but a solitary, unitary, central
aberrant, visionary I-don't-what
and-will-never-know-why
one eye.

*

Can we bury you in the normal graveyard
with the beloved we've loved and buried
to keep near? Will you desecrate the ground
or ascend like a singular star, blinking
one one one, from the loneliest place?

*

Is there double vision with one eye
better fore or hindsight?
Dead freak cat, are you a soothsayer
a harbinger, someone whose eyes crossed
so perfectly you couldn't tell them apart?
A cat who took symmetry too literally?

And, what and where is your heart?
A rouge globe, smack the center?

*

I can't cry for her lack of elegy.
She, the poet, was neither saving you
from the museum nor respecting
your strangeness. She was hiding you
because she was frightened
and ashamed of your birth
in a cradle of wasted eloquence.
They flash upon that inward eye
Which is the bliss of solitude.

But, the bones don't lie.
I'll dig them up, I swear
and you'll be there
to puzzle the archeologists
warn the farthest planets
and break our hearts.

*

What of the mother cat?
Where did she go
having given birth
to a crystal ball
that refused to tell?

SHE'S BEEN NAMED

Not that she didn't have a name before
an obscure (to Americans) French one
given by the elderly cat lady who died.

Then she was called *Calico* because
she's a calico, and *Tricolor* because
she's a French cat, and that's
what they call calicos.

But our loveliest neighbor
has given her the name of a flower (almost).
That they gave her a name at all
is the essential miracle.

She, a reticent calico with an obscure past
abandoned by death to the generic is now
Lillian.

I call her that with joy for another chance
(ignoring that lilies are poisonous to cats.)
Lillian. Good kitty. Girlfriend.
(Calicos are always female…)

I tried to befriend you for 2 years, but you fled.
Oh, I needed kitty love, and I came first!
But our neighbor was more generous

and now you're almost a friendly species
within your limits, in the context of proper
respect, allegiance to individuality.

When I was a kid, Fran the nurse who lived upstairs
and had great authority because she was a nurse
said, "Everyone is an individuality."

She's been named *Lillian*
almost like the flower
and so I know
she is loved.

Unfolding the Silence
(In Praise of Bats)

Why are you always blaming bats?
Their unique ability to terrify
especially now? But, consider, all
those nasty diseases they proffer—
lethal zoonotic zoonoses, corona
catastrophes—don't faze. Neither
rabies nor *rage* (apt in French).
We should be celebrating them!
Celebrating and inquiring how it's done.
Let's borrow, if not worship their skill.
They eat mosquitos, too.
They sleep, unfold their beautiful
paper-like wings, their long, strange
literary history, the silence when
they flutter after birds are asleep.

COMPARATIVE ANATOMY

Every part can be construed
as parallel, human, humanoid:
limbs, jaws, cute little noses.
Except the tail. What is *that?*

Once, a woman in the hospital
thought she had a one, a huge one
like an alligator or dinosaur.
It wasn't a question. She felt it
was there, knew it was there.

It was there! And she
a slender, delicate young woman
walked in great graceful lurches
to bear it, sometimes with her arms
curled to cradle it.

They say a tail is for balance.
In her case, it was unbalance.
None of the nurses or doctors
could see it, but who's to say
a delusion isn't the body's certainty?

*

When *the body* became
a precious post-modern term
my little cat didn't know it.

But he knows when he looks at me
and blinks that long, slow, agreeable
cat blink, that I am looking at him too
with eyes, through eyes, eye to eye.

When I stroke him, bliss unto
annoyance, and his tail goes *thunk*
does he notice I don't have one?

*

When I eat peanuts
I feel I'm an elephant, the slow wrinkled
sonorous body, trunk curling like the spiral
of a shooting star.

Not those salty, greasy barfly things
but real peanuts, in the beautiful
waffled shells. (What can they
possibly be made of?)

Roasted to nutty, a kind of ambrosia
the carmine skins slightly, pleasantly bitter
a little man's head inside with a French bow tie.

It ain't peanuts. How misguidedly maligned.
They are so, so good.

I feel the elephant's cylindrical saucer of a hoof
lifting, the body and gesture as if my own.

At sweet sixteen half a century ago
I cried for the elephants
walking and walking and finding
no water.

Everyone told me it was not about
the elephants, but my own sorrow.
They were wrong.

COQ AU VIN

As a child I thought it was *cocoa*.
(No idea about the *vin* yet, though.)

How is it that we learn? And, what
is this scent, tuberose? Intoxicating.

Or stranger, primrose, night blooming
cereus? How do we know what we know?

The slate roofs are silver when the sky is
or a blue so pale it may not even be a color.

How do we learn what sounds French
or what is hue, atmospheric, floral?

What is knowledge anyway?
Hearing or seeing, believing as if

wishes were truth, came true, but only
if you believe with all your heart.

Cocoa, what more fragrant a favorite
could there ever be? Chocolate or wine.

How do we learn to taste, to believe
to know reality: *It's a chicken!*

THE FISH GAZE

The first thing that happened, I started to feel
sorry for him (or her), that magnificent eye
so bright and lidless, a body so long he/she/they
hardly fit in the pan. So artistically stuffed to the gills
yes, literally of course, with beautiful herbs even
carrot tops. (Why waste what might be celebrated?)

Prepare to meet your maker, fish!

Prepare for death? Who can possibly prepare
or be prepared for death? This bright eye
had already been chosen by its maker, ogling
a reminder, guts gutted, scales shorn, my oven
only an afterthought to cloud the lens.

I might have eaten that ripe eye as in past
smoked whitefish, Ashkenazi gold
dismantled the head, yes, its soft bones
and secret crevices, nothing to squander.
Charlemagne (the cat) and I could have
put every morsel on the platter to easy rest.

But, I felt too sorry now for this bewitching
animal—yes, fish are animals—raised I believe
on a farm, a fish farm, tank, cage, an ocean
beyond imagination only a fish can dream.

Years ago my friend, a vegetarian before fashion
or urgency said, "Nothing with a face."
This fish had the face of a god or goddess.
(Why gender a fish? Easier just to say, 'the fish'.
But, he/she/they had a face to fulfill remembrance.)

Doesn't everyone, every living creature have a face?
Let me grow old enough to feel sorry for plants.

Yes, the first thing that happened, I started feeling
sorry for fish after years if not decades of touching
translucent fins. I wanted to breathe water
with them, flap and shimmer, all our faces known.

I started to feel sorry for whelks too, the majesty
of their spirals that come out whole when boiled.
I know there are faces in there somewhere.
And scallops' thousands of shimmering eyes.

I felt terribly sorry for him. He *was* very large
and, honestly, if by damnable convention
when you saw him you thought, *he.*

How large was he? Not a meter or a yard.
About the width of the oven and a little more.
I had to bend his tail to fit him in.

Nothing with a face.

What color was he? Sort of fish-colored, a silvery
slightly speckled gray. And, slender, a "bar"
a.k.a. European sea bass. Firm, white, tasty cachet.

The fishmonger had scaled him on request
but a few translucent disks remained, sharp as glass
removed by rubbing, like rubbing a cat the wrong way.

The dorsal fin was flat until you fanned it
lethal as an old world rose thorn. Beautiful teeth, yes
tinier than a child's. I wish I could have known him
when he was alive, to describe his serpentine wriggle.

But, is description ever more than the anatomy of
the describer? Face to face, I can hardly bear to look
the gaze now only my own self-centered eye.

CROWS
—for W.S. Merwin

He says he cried when he first saw them.
I believe him, and I know why.

I cry too, often.
Not always for or about crows.
Sometimes, just sorrow.
For injury, for loss, as well as awe.
Yes, awe.

Crows are of awe. Ha, they caw!
It's just that if you've never seen them
beyond Van Gogh, only imagined
or most of the rest of a world
so many neither see nor miss

a crow is a breath, a crazy cawing liberation
a flock of them, those smartie pies.
Who cares if they're called 'a murder'?

Was the world was better without *us*?
Or, better before our tools became toxic
along with our souls. Please
I grew up in a city, one of the biggest

please let me touch the satin wings.
Let ambition not kill us all.
Let something kind, even with a wink
be our lost nature.

He wept when he first saw crows
and I know why.

KNOWLEDGE

How do you know
when something is dead?
Infinitely obvious, one knows.

I see a story about a dog in the road
who was rescued.

But, the cat I saw...
Why remember now and have a fantasy?

It was not to be.
It was obviously no longer being.

How does one know with utter certainty?
Why did I want to rescue it?

You can rescue the living, maybe.
You cannot rescue the dead
or help but know the difference.

CLOSER THOUGHTS
for Eleni Rodis

Was it after a sad man came looking
after we saw a dead cat in the road, or
the slits for garlic slivers in the Easter lamb
that the straining cognitive dissonance collapsed?

Flesh became flesh. In France I reviled in disgust
at *cheval* in the market. Rabbits are the only
trilogy of garden pest, pet and table fare.

As a little girl I went fishing with my dad, but
at some point saw they couldn't breathe in air.
Then, as I said, I started feeling sorry for whelk/
conch/scungilli, the throwaway nobody wanted.

My friend had said, "Nothing with a face."
But, once I began to pluck them out of the sea
the scallops had eyes, rows of them, glimmering
as they chattered in protest of their demise.

Every one and every thing has eyes within.

OK, I'm to blame for having domesticated you.
Will you take a home, straw and grain in exchange
for milk and eggs? Honey is always stolen, though.

A woo-woo friend said it's alright, some blood types
need meat. I supposed I was one, whichever it is.

Cats need, dogs need, lions and tigers and polar bears
frogs and snakes, spiders and sharks, our gentle friend
the octopus, penguin pals, sea gulls, crocodiles and
many more are all obligate, as in obligatory carnivores.

As a Pisces I thought, well, we understand each other
if I eat a fish or a fish eats me, it's the same thing.
(I made that up to keep the cognitive dissonance at bay.)

And now the NYT says someone is eating song birds.
(The newspaper that resembles the National Enquirer
of my childhood. The world that resembles...)
Perhaps those who eat them will sing.

Some cultures, though few, eat cat. Can I imagine
sinewy and bitter, obstinate, whom I rejoice
in being chosen by?
Who to feed to whom?
Fish or fowl? Dog or dog meat?
My strange omnivore husband one day
asked if vegetables feel pain. Then said
"I suspect they do."

CAT

To those on Facebook who think
they'll see their dead cats again
across 'the rainbow bridge' one day:
No, I don't think so, but how much
I love you, and understand how much
you love your cats. I've loved and love
my cats, not as humans, but as cats
as if I were a cat, or have needed
to be a cat, a creature with a creature's
heart. I love and understand, and sigh
for your perhaps loneliness, and thank
you for existing in this crazy world
saving kittens from road sacks
bottle-feeding dumpster fur-balls
every 2 hours 'round the clock
for days, inventing an online kitty
language we all understand. Some of
you are fat, some 'on the spectrum'
others politically...*I can't I can't I can't.*
But can, CAT. I know they're just
cats. I know I can replace even the most
beloved one, and have, after rivers
of tears, and love the next, and the next
learning each time, so many cats, so
little time. But, it's you I love
the most for loving them so much.
You, the human, whose heart
has been shattered, whose earth
has been ravaged, if not destroyed.
And now, uncalled, he's arrived
the little black *fumé* (that's smoke)
guy. We're attached at the soul
though no such thing exists
in either of our universes.

OVER

It was that image
and a man out searching
for what I'd seen.

Now, it's us. Cats
die accidently, bizarrely.
My little bunny.

Let's get it over with:
He died. Yes, I cried
and cried and cried.

and am still crying.

None of all the terrible
things I worried about.
A different sudden

accidental turn.
Turn the clock back.
Nine lives is nothing.

All loss like a hollow
gasp of breath
unheard.

Does sorrow wash
does sorrow melt
does it end?

All sorrow, sorrows
wash, cleanse
leave stay

swept hearth
put away away away
practice for the real

thing *after the first*
so long ago
who will curl

right hand or left
conjoint fur
aimless reaching.

He was looking for me I know
and died without knowing
I'd return.

I want to rush grief
beyond the slow melt
in the middle of the night.

My little friend
boyfriend, as I called you
loathing the idea

of calling a cat a child
silly heart, purity
bless the next in line.

I Go to Lascaux

I go to Lascaux
for truth and more
importantly, meaning.

I go to what is now faux
to preserve the original.
Faux Lascaux.

What were they trying
to tell us? That there
were beasts? And, each

that did not yet have
an arrow in its heart
would eventually.

V

THE POETS

And they grow old
and say all their words
about their lives
about saying words
about their lives.

What worth?

And they take the pulse
or are the pulse
of history, telemetric
suffusion of
the inevitable.

Many ways to love
words and many ways
to hate them. They
get in the way.

The Problem with Poetry

Too many words
or too few. Images
but why, imagination?
Who cares if or what you
can imagine? Or feel.
Just because you've had
a feeling and are human do
you have to write it down?
Like a teenager saying they
have a 'chemical imbalance'
when no, it just 'an emotion'.
Expression, to express
as in pus from a wound?
Or, to celebrate the sky
sea, trees, love. Why
does even very eloquent
language sound generic?
I must be old. Hey, I am
old. Try that on for reprise.

Inside a Cloud

They allow you to bring yourself
deeply into them. *Brouillard.*
An image won't do, it has to be
imagined—the depth, the sensation
warm and cool at the same time.

Description is unfathomable.
Renegade *renégate* re-negate negate create.
Languages try and try, with some
success. Music is better for transport.

Once inside, there is no body, all sound
is hollow but resonant, and full. Touch
is complete, or a complete abstraction.
There's nothing to see. Try to see
something ineffable.

ARS POETICA

That's a nice poem, but we're trying for literature here.
—Michael Klein

What is poetry, anyway?
Years ago a friend wrote a line
"Something something—I forget
what—*stirs the bitter raven."*
(Perhaps we were all children of Poe.)

But I got the wicked giggles and it
mutated to "stir-fries the bitter raven."
…still makes me laugh, kinda mean
but not meant to be. It was a question.
What the Hell is poetry anyway?

Is it being? Is it freedom? Is it about
hearing or saying? Feeling, of course.
Is that the same as meaning?
Philosophy? *(Please…)* Being lost
or found? A diver, an asteroid, a suicide?

What pulse can be taken? What
listening to what murmur or thunder
or song or wail? What can you tell
the world? Of annihilation? Swimming?

Tell *elegance* to stay or go? Peel the skin
off the frog, sit inside the whale.
Make sense when none is there.
Nonsense because language
is a lost heartbeat, hoofbeat, drum.

Now I'm going to write some life
and death lines about life and death.
Now *the pitiless wave*. Now I'm going
to look for a recipe for the eggplant
that's going bad. The gift of language.

Experience is transient and cannot
be one thing with conviction that cannot
be one thing, that cannot
help but apologize for itself.

In Translation

Language has a peculiar ability to translate itself
free-associating like a patient in psychoanalysis.

My friend Sherry loved studying French in High School
because she could be a different person, more fluid in her

adolescent bones, more flirtatious, well, more *French*.
The thesaurus knows, searching and searching

how luxurious and opulence, indulgence
are suddenly lush, luxuriant, soon to revel.

And, now I am transported to a city in Egypt.
Who am I in Luxor, my tongue dancing?

Another friend asks, "Is *desire* the same as *yearning*?"
Utterly meaningless, but for the psyche that loves chic.

Ah, the action of desire, the post-modern fetish of desire
the magnificent foreign city, the ancient foreign self.

GOT SCISSORS, GOT CÆSURAE

It was during Covid, so yes, I cut it myself.
Don't accuse me of having gone to the beauty parlor
before or after curfew. And, think I may continue—
frizzy is forgiving.

Paused and broke the lines myself, too.
They broke where they may, and I was free
or irresponsible, not responsible, for hair or poem.
One will grow back, the other
who cares?

Remembering Ferlinghetti

Was it *ontology* or *ontogeny*?
And, which one recapitulates
phylogeny?

I would have written sooner
if I'd remembered you were still
alive. And now it's too late.
101 years too late.

What else can't I remember
other than once upon a time
when poems and even poets
and the universe was full
of lighthearted good cheer?

CONFESSIONAL

I shall not use "I".
No "I" ever again
not even as an aside
(maybe a persona).

It shall not be
a diary, a journal, a log
anything personal
unless universal.

The personal is political.
And, that is true
more than you know
in our post-modern
relativistic semblance
of...

what? Being, self?
Original only in as much
as there was an origin
of the species.

I shall not use "I"
but "you" to hear from
you, your sorrow
at least for a while.

The political is personal
too. How pain breaks
from state to hand, speaks
en masse without water
or only water to drown in.

Refuge from where
to where? There used
to be a place to land.

SPEECH

I think I hear someone speaking
but it's the wind. It really is—
the chimney's a mouth

with wind across it
indistinguishable from speech.

Time is short. I don't have time
to learn anything. I learn something
every day.

There's a cacophony
of voices—steam escaping
the tea kettle, a volatile dove.

What's being said?
I listen, halt and listen again
and again. Rilke's destiny?

No, just the mouth
of a chimney with sooty lungs
saying what it will, anything

you want it to say
uncensored, unabridged

indistinguishable
from the cadence of thought
halting punctuation of thought.

RHYME

I am going to make
a white asparagus *velouté*.
Connaissez? And
for a French friend
(who could care less
by the way).

Because they're in season
those beautiful, *cher* things
grown in hummocks
of dirt, not easy to peel.

My friend is neither a foodie
nor keen on the French. Why
do we turn our skepticism
toward our own, and all
but worship the other?

Things French in particular
for example. Why is fantasy
(or, conspiracy theory)
stronger than reality?

Rhyme is inescapable
and embarrasses me as do
questions unto infinity.

I rhyme because…
I don't expect to understand.
I rhyme because I can.
I rhyme to listen and to hear
Emily speak of a mouse for
happiness and confidence
we're not alone in the universe.

FOR ADRIENNE RICH

It's taken so long to grasp
what has always been in reach
gift, birthright

the vote during reconstruction
poignantly arrived for
with baskets in hand.

It's taken a long time
for voice beyond plea
to trust the hand.

            *

You were off to the stratosphere
visionary, obvious.

I was making a ragged escape
from the madhouse

in the clouds, looking for a safe place.
What clouds? Some clouds.

A child making an earthen cubby
in which to put unidentified berries

for consolation and show
doubtless inedible.

I didn't know I was allowed
to take myself seriously.

            *

Oh there were other sorrows
en route to old age, nearly a lifetime
to come home to you

to be able to be almost
as patient and generous
with myself as you.

Words swam on the page.
I barely saw them
or knew what they meant.

But I knew you so well
the way only an arrogant girl
in search of her rightful home could.

Lauri, you want a mother and I
don't want a daughter. I am my daughter.
All the better for both of us.

No gesture escaped, note
of voice, corporeality, laugh as if
a child remembering everything:

The cat you held at the door
to prevent escape, a beautiful
young boy, the shyest witness.

The cigarettes we smoked
as normal pleasure
back in those days.

I knew your kindness
in a small room, when poets
sat in small rooms.

I watched you scale
the stratosphere, visionary beyond
necessity, or even destiny

afraid to continue to speak
I thought, to you
but it was to myself.

*

Lacking a skill is not the same
as being impaired.

Being fearful may or may
not be an impairment.

Fear itself may or may not be.
Kindness is almost never.

You treated me as a peer
of sorts, took me seriously.

You called me a warrior
"a warrior filled with love"

when I was merely the daughter
of a mad woman, and filled with fear.

*

You were on a mission to always be
on a mission, each worthy
of tearing the cloth.

A warrior filled with love.

Now you're owned by still living
history, though history will never
know how truly kind you were.

Vesuvius, the clock still ticks...

It is not a language of pain
that is visionary, plainspoken
and held quietly.

I met a boy trying to teach himself
to read. He was determined
but said *deter-mined*.

Each word came as it came
from where and whom ever it came
learning like that intrepid kid

determined to remake bedrock
shift it anew, discover all gifts
as if they had not been given.

You took yourself seriously
became the self you took seriously.
You were deter-mined.

Arabesque

OK, is it time
to let some lyric back in
or something imagistic?
Is it possible

to break the narrative
of pure grief, consternation
and vain annoyance
for a world depriving us
of a 'peaceful' old age.

I return to the crows
Is it possible?

They're smarter than we.
Let me try: Their beautiful
black wings, like shattered
obsidian. Their thoughts—

are they as kind as they are
clever, the centuries wonder.
Their loft above the fields'
perfection, their busy array
on the ground, like tiny priests
no worse than charming

unless you're the farmer.
They do not 'murder'
unless you're the dreamer.

Old age was never meant
to be peaceful—bones
to consider, fragile as bird wings
blue-black veins. Forgetting how

even to say goodbye, far across
the field, as the crow flies
as the last rhyme reminds.

Who in the piebald universe
is ready for this? Where is
the majestic obsidian bird?

SUMMER IS NICE

Summer is nice.
It warms the face.
Summer and grace.
Don't let it sound
only sing-song.
Summer can be
a minor ecstasy if
you stop the rhyme
embrace the light
with gravity *(oops)*.

What is it language
allows us and fails
to divulge, a longing
to touch the far away
season within, beyond
the sun, of merely
sitting on the balcony
a little while, light
crossing one's eyelids
as if touch, rendering
the story of who
we really are.

Après-Après
(Addendum February 2022)

I'll take you into my arms
my home, my heart, if
you are still alive. We can
learn each other's languages
if we still have tongues.

If there are words to tear
a hole in the universe
through which to escape
or return. From shatter to shatter.

Perhaps we deserve ourselves
our species of villains, perhaps
the righteous too, the last
invasion of wanton greed
immolation as if reason.

They called WWI *The Great War*
until there was another. Then it had
a number. The 2nd killed my tribe
and many others. The 3rd will be

The Last.

NOTES

I

For Ten in Salbris
We wanted to love, and loved / *false or true*, allusion W.B. Yeats, "When You are Old".
...*weep that I was every born*. Allusion to E.A. Robinson, "Miniver Cheevy".

The Secret Garden
Substance – *Pile the bodies high... Shovel them under...* Carl Sandburg, "Grass".
...*Who made him dead to rapture and despair, /A thing that grieves not and that never hopes...* Edwin Markham, "The Man With the Hoe".
...*What dread hand? & what dread feet? /What the hammer? what the chain?* William Blake, "The Tyger".
Lola – *The Sin-eaters*: https://en.wikipedia.org/wiki/Sin-eater
the grave you dig for me...where...long to be. Robert Lewis Stevenson, "Requiem".
Mama – *nevermore...never again*. Allusions to Edgar Allen Poe, "The Raven" and The Holocaust.
"I want to touch the world." George Floyd, https://www.nytimes.com/article/george-floyd-who-is.html
Woke – *Is there water? Troubled?* Allusion to Ramsey Lewis, song, "Wade in the Water".
Beyond – *Send their dogs to bite our bodies.* Gil Turner, song, "Carry it On".

White to Black
I thought of all the children coming forever and ever into the world, white, with the black shadow already falling upon them before they draw breath. William Faulkner, *Light in August*.

Mouzieys-Panens 2020
Forgive me [   ]... Allusion to William Faulkner's use of blank spaces in *As I Lay Dying*.
Godless Jew... Allusion to Peter Gay's monograph on Sigmund Freud, *A Godless Jew*.
Stone walls do not a prison make nor iron bars a cage. Richard Lovelace, "To Althea from Prison".
"I was more interesting than they were." Toni Morrison, documentary film.

The Pieces I Am.
Tell all the truth but...tell it slant... Emily Dickinson, #1263.
the bit. Reference to Toni Morrison, *Beloved.*

What Makes you Think
 Only half of London died in 1348. Reference to the bubonic plague.

A Stand of Trees
Why don't I *know* more about *something.* Echo of Elizabeth Bishop, "Why
didn't I know enough of something?" "Crusoe in England".
Tenants that neither speak nor stir / Yet dwell in mute insistence. Adrienne
Rich, "Toward the Solstice".

I Hear That Those Who Cannot...
The Met... The Metropolitan Opera.
They speak a vision of their own heart, Jeremiah 23:16.

Inaugural
Joe Biden and Kamala Harris, January 20, 2021.

Spring
For what purpose, April, do you return...cruelest month. References to Edna St.
Vincent Millay, "Spring" and T.S. Eliot, "The Waste Land"

II

Cookbook
Maya Kaimal Macmillan, *Curried Favors: Family Recipes from South India.*
If *there's nothing left now but the food and the humor...* Adrienne Rich, "Sources, XVII".

What I Wish I'd Studied
Don't know much about history. Sam Cooke song, "Wonderful World".
Reference to Edith Hamilton, *Mythology.*

House Philosophy
 ...inward eye. Tacit reference to William Wordsworth, "I Wandered Lonely
as a Cloud".

Let Us Now Praise…
Walker Evans, Library of Congress: https://www.loc.gov/item/2002708957/
https://waihora-gallery.com/what-happened-to-lucille-burroughs/
James Agee, *Let Us Now Praise Famous Men*

How Tired
What is poetry which does not save /Nations or people? Czeslaw Milosz,
"Dedication"
tell all the truth… Echo of Emily Dickinson, #1263.

Admonition
To be or not to be… Wm. Shakespeare, *Hamlet*.

Anorexic
Helen Keller grabbing scrambled eggs in her palm. Katharine E. Wilkie, *Helen Keller: From Tragedy to Triumph*.

Dear Sarah,
one life, Echo of Mary Oliver, "The Summer Day".

III

Birthday Poems
let evening come… Jane Kenyon (who died in her 40's of cancer) "Let Evening Come"

Already Living
Change your life. Allusion to Rainer Maria Rilke, "Archaic Torso of Apollo".

Coming of Aging
Not Erikson's *integrity vs. despair*: https://en.wikipedia.org/wiki/Erik_Erikson

Shabby
Reference to "Toxic Squash Syndrome": https://en.wikipedia.org/wiki/Cucurbitacin

Paresthesias
E.A. Robinson, "Miniver Cheevy".

Old Woman's Body
Why / should aging de-recapitulate ontogeny? Reference to Recapitulation theory: https://en.wikipedia.org/wiki/Recapitulation_theory

Dementia
...*something in me understands /the voice...* e.e. cummings, "somewhere i have never traveled, gladly beyond".
...the dancer with dementia /rising like a swan: https://www.npr.org/2020/11/10/933387878/struck-with-memory-loss-a-dancer-remembers-swan-lake-but-who-is-she?t=1646677160321

IV

The Cat Went Out
I turned and looked the other way / and saw...three islands in a bay; To what purpose, April, do you return again? Edna St. Vincent Millay, "Renascence" and "Spring".

Cyclops Cap in Six Riffs
Reference to Mary Oliver, "The Kitten".
They flash upon that inward eye / Which is the bliss of solitude. William Wordsworth, "I Wandered Lonely as a Cloud".

Comparative Anatomy
In reference to elephant populations, for example: https://www.worldwildlife.org/magazine/issues/winter-2018/articles/the-status-of-african-elephants

The Fish Gaze
A fish tale: After I wrote the poem, minus the last stanza, I happened to read Elizabeth Bishop's "The Fish" to my husband who commented that it was self-centered. "How can it be self-centered?" I asked, "It's about a fish!" He disagreed, saying it's about the poet's absorption with her own attention to detail.

Crows
Reference to Vincent Van Gogh's painting, "Wheatfield with Crows"

Closer Thoughts
Reference to eating songbirds, for example: https://www.nytimes.com/2021/04/20/world/europe/italy-lunch-songbirds.html?searchResultPosition=2

Over
*…swept hearth…put away…*allusion to Emily Dickinson, 1108.
*…after the first…*allusion to Dylan Thomas, "A Refusal to Mourn the Death, by Fire, of a Child in London".
I Go to Lascaux
See, for example: https://www.npr.org/sections/parallels/2017/01/02/507549682/next-to-the-original-france-replicates-prehistoric-cave-paintings?t=1646824760950

V

Ars Poetica
Allusion to Edgar Allen Poe, "The Raven"; *the pitiless wave… a surf tormented shore…* "A Dream Within a Dream".

Remembering Ferlinghetti
https://www.nytimes.com/2021/02/23/obituaries/lawrence-ferlinghetti-dead.html
Reference to Lawrence Ferlinghetti, "Dog".

Confessional
The personal is political. https://en.wikipedia.org/wiki/The_personal_is_political

Speech
Rilke reportedly heard the first line of the 1st Duino Elegy in the wind: https://en.wikipedia.org/wiki/Duino_Elegies

Rhyme
Reference to Emily Dickinson, #793.

For Adrienne Rich
…tearing the cloth. Reference to a tradition of Jewish mourners.
Vesuvius, the clock still ticks… Reference to Adrienne Rich's essay on Emily Dickinson. "Vesuvius at Home", *Parnassus poetry in review,* Vol. 5, No. 1, 1976.

Arabesque
Who in the piebald universe… faint allusion to Gerard Manley Hopkins, "Pied Beauty".

LAURI ROBERTSON has written poetry for many years—
Adrienne Rich was her mentor. *Après*, or "After", referring
to the convergence of the pandemic and #BLM is her
4th monograph. Lauri is a psychiatrist / psychoanalyst
formerly on the clinical faculty of Yale Medical School.
She lives in New Haven, CT and Pontlevoy, France.

www.ingramcontent.com/pod-product-compliance
Lightning Source LLC
Chambersburg PA
CBHW011215120626
46545CB00008B/3004